T0381044

# HEALTHY COOK BOOK

### Guide to Healthy Eating, Lose 20 Pounds in Just 21 Days

EDITH BRAIMOH

Balboa Press books may be ordered through booksellers or by contacting:

Balboa Press
A Division of Hay House
1663 Liberty Drive
Bloomington, IN 47403
www.balboapress.com
1 (877) 407-4847

ISBN: 978-1-9822-1951-2 (sc)
ISBN: 978-1-9822-1952-9 (e)

Print information available on the last page.

Balboa Press rev. date: 11/29/2019

**BALBOA**.PRESS
A DIVISION OF HAY HOUSE

# The Truth About This Healthy Cook Book

The fact is that what is written in this cook book are years of research that I have done. They are what I have used, and they worked for me, my family and multitudes of others. Follow it precisely, that is the only way it will yield result.

If you want to eat healthy and live healthy, or you are struggling to lose weight, belly fat, experiencing hot flashes due to menopause, hypertension, high cholesterol, nephrotic syndrome, generalized pain, fibroid and cyst?

Visit our website to purchase a copy of this book and register in our program at www.ultragc. com and subscribe for once weekly email update.

# Acknowledgment

I give thanks to God Almighty for the strength and grace that He has bestowed upon me and, the inspiration to be able to write this book. I want to thank God for Pastor Dr. Lucky Braimoh, my husband, my pastor, my best friend, for his continuous support, love, and contribution which he has given me in writing this book. What can I do without you, honey? You have really been a blessing to me. Thanks for encouraging me to where God wants me to be. May the good Lord uphold you till the very end.

Thanks to my three lovely God-given children, Anavami, Ozavize and Omeiza for your love, patience, and support for mommy. I love you all. Thanks to my in-laws and my extended family for their prayer and support. And to everyone in RCCG, worldwide who supported me in one way or the other, God bless you all.

# Introduction

What's good for your body is essential for your taste buds! The recipes in this cookbook are what I have use myself and it show that you don't have to lose flavor to eat nutritious foods. Eating and staying healthy can be a stressful, but lifestyle changes like eating healthy, living healthy and staying healthy can help lower your risk for heart disease and other health issues.

You know what, one way to eat a healthy diet is to choose a variety of foods. Variety is key, because no food has all the nutrients that your heart and your entire body need. A healthy eating plan is the one that emphasize on fruits, vegetables, whole grains, fat-free or low-fat milk, plant milk, like almond milk, soy milk, lean meats, poultry, fish, beans, eggs, and nuts. It is low in saturated fat, *trans* fat, cholesterol, sodium, and added sugars. What you drink also matters, drinking 8 cups of water daily, herbal tea. Choose nonalcoholic, low/no-calorie options such as water, skim milk, iced tea, and sparkling beverages as a substitute for regular, sweetened beverages.

Eating healthy involves portion size and the timing of your food. The recipes in this cookbook are designed to give you a satisfying portion, while helping you stay within your calorie limits.

The recipes in this cookbook also are limited in fat, saturated fat, *trans* fat, cholesterol, sodium, and calories. They use lean cuts of meat, poultry without the skin, fish, beans, whole grains, fruits, vegetables, small amounts of vegetable oil, and lots of herbs and spices for flavor. Most of all, these recipes are delicious. For more information on how to shop for, prepare, and serve healthy meals, visit us at www.ultrahealthyliving.org, follow us on Facebook, twitter and histogram.

*We hope you will enjoy the recipes in this cookbook*

# Tips for Becoming a Good Cook

CLEAN KITCHEN

Strive to start your cooking with a clean kitchen. Having a clear counter will help you have a clear mind. As a cook, clean after your self. You need to create a good standard of hygiene and appearance.

Make sure your hair is cover when cooking.

BE ORGANIZED

Before cooking, declutter your pantry. Organization begin now. Watch my video on YouTube on how to organize your pantry. Throw away expired items. Get clean jars with label to organize your pantry. Take out the equipment you need for cooking. Make them as accessible as you can. Before you start cooking. Get a shopping list, purchase all the items for the cooking. Avoid overloading the counter. Place all your cooking supply in one basket on your counter top. Finally, clean after yourself as you cook.

CONFIDENCE

It is ok to be afraid of how your food will taste after cooking or make mistake, make your mistakes and learn from it, keep practicing and experimenting until you are able to build up your confidence. Confidence is being in control of what you do, once you make your mistakes in cooking, for instance adding too much salt or pepper or using the wrong recipe, do not condemn yourself, most people do that, such people easily give up and they give up in cooking. Please learn from it and then move on. This attitude will make you a better cook eventually.

PRESENTATION

Cooking is all about creativity, the presentation of your food is very important, it makes the food attractive. You should present your food using your own imagination as long as it looks pleasing to the eye. Food should be neatly served.

TEACHABLE HEART

Do not assume you know it all. Please learn to take correction when you make mistakes and, when you are given constructive feedback. Never fail to listen to their corrections and don't get angry, this will help you a lot. Make sure you ask questions on how the food looks, or taste.

PRESERVATION

Make sure you use fresh or well-preserved ingredients when cooking. Your perishable goods can be kept in your deep refrigerator;

# Chapter 1

# APPETIZERS

# Healthy Baguette Bread Appetizers

## INGREDIENTS

- ➢ 7 ripe tomatoes
- ➢ 2 cloves garlic, chopped
- ➢ 1 Tbsp 100% extra virgin olive oil
- ➢ 1 teaspoon balsamic vinegar

- ➢ 6 chopped fresh basil leaves
- ➢ 2 pinched of sea salt to taste
- ➢ ½ teaspoon black pepper
- ➢ 1 baguette or Italian bread or 100% wheat bread

## DIRECTIONS

1. Finely chop the tomatoes and place them in a medium bowl.

2. Mix in the minced garlic, 1 Tbsp 100% extra virgin olive oil, and the balsamic vinegar.

3. Stir in the thinly sliced basil and add salt to taste and black pepper.

# Egg Mimosa

## INGREDIENTS

- ➤ 4 large eggs
- ➤ 2 to 3tsps mayonnaise
- ➤ Pinch of curry powder
- ➤ Salt and pepper to season

- ➤ 1/2 green onion nicely chopped
- ➤ I tablespoon of chopped parsley leaves
- ➤ Sprinkling of little paprika

## DIRECTION

1. Put eggs in a pot of cold water, set it on the stove, and bring to the boil uncovered. As soon as you see bubbles, turn off heat. Drain the eggs and put them under cold running water and peel.

2. Halve the eggs and remove the yolks. Mash them with the mayonnaise and curry powder to taste. Season with salt and pepper, and a little chopped green onion. Stuff the whites with the yolk mixture and arrange on a serving platter. Remember to garnish with paprika and parsley leaves

# Shrimp Stuffed Cucumber Cups Recipe

## INGREDIENTS

- ➤ Use kosher salt
- ➤ 2 pounds medium-small shrimp, peeled
- ➤ 8 organic limes, juiced
- ➤ 8 organic lemons, juiced
- ➤ 2 organic oranges, juiced, preferably sour oranges
- ➤ 2 large organic tomatoes, cut into 1/2-inch dice
- ➤ 1 red organic onion, nicely chopped
- ➤ 1 bunch cilantro, nicely chopped
- ➤ 1 serrano chile, nicely chopped
- ➤ 2 large avocados, peeled, cut into cubes
- ➤ 1 large cucumber, peeled and cut into half

## DIRECTIONS

1. In a large pot of boiling salted water, add the shrimp about 5 minutes.

2. Drain the shrimp, cut into 1-inch pieces, and transfer to a bowl. Add the lime, lemon, and orange juice, stir to combine, and refrigerate for at least 2 hours.

3. Stir the tomato, onion, cilantro, and chile into the shrimp mixture and let sit at room temperature for about 20 minutes

4. When ready to serve, gently stir in the avocado and cucumber.

# Buffalo Chicken Wings with Homemade Blue Cheese Dressing

## INGREDIENTS

- ➢ 1/2 teaspoons kosher salt
- ➢ 2 teaspoons paprika
- ➢ 1 teaspoon cayenne pepper
- ➢ 1 teaspoon onion powder
- ➢ 1 teaspoon garlic powder
- ➢ 3/4 teaspoon white pepper

- ➢ 10 tablespoons coconut or olive oil
- ➢ 1 tablespoon plus 1 teaspoon Tabasco sauce
- ➢ 24 chicken wings
- ➢ 2 cups vegetable oil
- ➢ Blue cheese dressing (recipe follows)
- ➢ celery or carrot sticks (optional)

### *Blue Cheese Dressing Recipe*

- ➢ 2 eggs
- ➢ 1 tablespoon fresh lemon juice
- ➢ 1 tablespoon apple cider vinegar

- ➢ 1/4 cup chopped onions
- ➢ 1/4 cup chopped celery
- ➢ 1/2 teaspoon salt

**DIRECTIONS**

1. Thoroughly combine the salt, paprika, cayenne, onion powder, garlic powder and pepper in a small bowl.

2. Melt 5 tablespoons of coconut or olive oil with 2 teaspoons of the Tabasco sauce in a small saucepan over low heat.

3. Pour into a small shallow bowl and allow it cool.

4. Put the chicken wings into a large bowl and coat well with 2 tablespoons of the seasoning mix.

5. Add the butter/Tabasco mixture and work in well with your hands until chicken is completely coated, and seasonings are well distributed.

6. Set aside to marinate for up to 30 minutes, covered and heat the oil.

7. Heat the oil over high heat until it is very hot.

8. Add the chicken wings, fitting in as many as there is room for in a single layer.

9. Fry until crisp and golden brown, about 8 to 12 minutes, turning several times.

10. Drain on paper towels.

11. Repeat with the remaining wings.

12. Serve with blue cheese dressing and celery sticks, if desired.

# Iceberg Wedge Salad with "Ranch" Dressing

## INGREDIENTS

- 1/2 cup greek yogurt
- 1 Tablespoon finely chopped chives
- 1 garlic clove, finely grated or minced
- salt and pepper to taste
- 1/2 head of iceberg lettuce, cut into 4 wedges (slices)
- 2 Tablespoons finely sliced green onions (scallions)
- 2 Tablespoons finely diced red bell pepper
- 2 Tablespoons pumpkin seeds (salted is just fine!)
- 1/8 teaspoon smoked paprika

## DIRECTIONS

1. Combine the first four ingredients to make the imitation/low-fat/faux ranch dressing. Mix well and then depending on consistency, add up to 1-1/2 Tablespoons water to thin it out to make it more like a dressing, but don't make it runny. When I make it, it's not pourable and yes, I made up that word. Season to taste.

2. Plate all 4 wedges on a serving dish and spoon the dressing evenly over each quarter, on the cut side of the wedge.

3. Sprinkle each wedge with green onions, red bell pepper, and pumpkin seeds.

4. Garnish with a generous pinch of smoked paprika on each wedge.

## RECIPE FOR RANCH DRESSING

- ➢ One of cup buttermilk
- ➢ Half cup sour cream
- ➢ Half cup whole egg mayonnaise
- ➢ 1 Tbsp. of lemon juice
- ➢ 2 cloves of mashed garlic

- ➢ 1 tsp dried dill
- ➢ 1 Tbsp chopped chives
- ➢ Half teaspoon of kosher salt
- ➢ Black pepper 1 -1/2 iceberg lettuce cut into 6 wedges

## METHODS

1. In bowl, put all dressing ingredients and whisk until the mixture becomes smooth. Transfer into another container and refrigerate. To serve, nicely place the lettuce on a plate and put the dressing on the side. Ready to eat.

# Shrimp & Avocado Cucumber Rolls

## INGREDIENTS

- 10 cooked, thawed shrimp
- 1 Tablespoon of coconut oil
- 1 large garlic clove, peeled and minced
- 1/2 of an avocado, peeled and pitted

- 2 Tablespoons chopped basil leaves
- 1 Tablespoon freshly squeezed lemon juice
- 2 English cucumbersIn a bowl combine the sauce ingredients until smooth.

## DIRECTIONS

1. Place a cucumber slice in front of you and spread a teaspoon of the sauce on the cucumber.

2. Press an avocado slice into the sesame seeds on both sides.

3. Place the avocado and shrimp on tops of the cucumber slice and tightly, but gently roll the cucumber

4. Repeat for remaining ingredients.

5. Serve with remaining sau

# Chapter 2

# BREAKFAST

**HEALTHY BREAKFAST RECIPE**

Pancake and Egg

Chicken Sandwich

Oatmeal

Waffles

Sprouted Wheat Cereal Apple Breakfast

Raw Granola

Fruit Shaker

**ENJOY THE BREAKFST!**

# Pancake and Eggs Breakfast

## INGREDIENTS

- 1 Cup All Purpose Flour or wheat flower or gluten free flower
- 1 Teaspoon honey
- 1/4 Teaspoon Ground Cinnamon
- 2 Teaspoons Baking Powder
- 1/4 Teaspoon Salt1 Cup almond Milk
- 1 Tablespoon olive or coconut Oil
- 1 Tablespoon Water
- 1 Teaspoon Vanilla Extract
- 2 Tablespoons Butter

## DIRECTIONS

1. Whisk together the dry ingredients.

2. In a liquid measuring mug, measure 1 cup milk. To that add the olive or coconut oil, water and vanilla extract.

3. Stir in the wet ingredients to the dry ingredients. Do not over-mix. Lumps are perfectly fine. Set aside for a couple of minutes.

4. Heat a griddle at medium-high heat. Once the pan is hot add the butter and let it melt.

5. Add the melted butter to the pancake batter and return the pan to the stove. Mix the butter into the batter.

6. When the pan is hot enough, pour a ladleful of batter on the pan for each pancake. Cook until bubbles appear on the face of the pancake. Carefully flip the pancake and cook until its golden brown. You can add blue berries fruits if you like. Yummy

# Healthy Chicken Sandwich

## INGREDIENTS

- ½ cauliflower
- 3 medium-sized carrots
- 2 bell peppers
- 2 cups, cooked chicken (cubed)
- ½ cup, mayonnaise
- 1 tablespoon, lemon juice

- Black pepper and salt - as per taste
- ¼ cup, ripe olives
- ¼ cup, chili sauce
- ¼ cup, parsley
- ½ cup, French green beans

## DIRECTIONS

1. Slice the cauliflower, carrots, green beans, and bell pepper finely and cook them. While the vegetables are being cooked, mix the mayonnaise, chili sauce, lemon juice, salt, and pepper together, in a bowl. Let the cooked vegetables cool and put them into the chicken bowl and toss. Pour the mixture in it and mix well. Spread on any kind of bread and serve.

# Oatmeal Breakfast

## INGREDIENTS

- ➤ 2 cups water or almond milk
- ➤ 1 cup old fashioned oatmeal
- ➤ 10 blueberries
- ➤ 5 slices of strawberries

- ➤ 5 raspberries
- ➤ 3 black berries
- ➤ 5 slices of banana
- ➤ 1 teaspoon honey

## DIRECTIONS

1. In a medium sauce pan combine the almond milk, oatmeal, and maple syrup, heat on low until most of the milk is absorbed (stir as needed), once most of the milk is absorbed and it has cool down, add in all the fruits and stir together. It is ready to serve.

# Waffles

## INGREDIENTS

- ➢ 1 ½ cups of whole wheat flour
- ➢ 2 teaspoons baking powder
- ➢ ½ teaspoon of salt
- ➢ 3 tablespoons of honey

- ➢ 1 large egg
- ➢ 1 ½ cups of almond milk
- ➢ ⅓ cup of olive oil

## DIRECTIONS

1. Preheat your iron while you make the waffle batter.

2. Whisk together the flour, baking powder, salt, and sugar.

3. In a separate bowl, whisk together the egg, milk, and oil.

4. Mix together the wet and dry ingredients, stirring just until combined. The batter will be a bit lumpy; that's OK.

# Sprouted Wheat Cereal Recipe

## INGREDIENTS

- 2 cups sprouted wheat
- 4 cups spring or filtered water
- 1/2 cup raisins
- 1 large apple, peeled, cored or 1 banana peeled and sliced

## DIRECTIONS

1. Soak raisins in one cup of the spring or filtered water for one hour or until soft. Reserve the water used in soaking the raisins. In a blender, blend wheat with fruit, water and raisin soakwater at medium speed for about two minutes. Use alkaline water or warm filtered water if a warm cereal is desired. The sprouted wheat cereal should have a soupy consistency. Sprouted (hulled) buckwheat, sunflower seeds, or sesame seeds may be substituted for the wheat. (All seeds should be soaked at least 6 hours or overnight.)

# Apple Breakfast Recipe

## INGREDIENTS

- ➢ 1 Large unpeeled apple
- ➢ Diced
- ➢ ¾ Cup rolled oats
- ➢ ¼ Cup maple syrup
- ➢ ½ Cup chopped walnuts

- ➢ 1 Cup soy yogurt
- ➢ 2 tbsp wheat germ
- ➢ Ground cinnamon (optional)
- ➢ Ground nutmeg (optional)

## DIRECTIONS

1. In a bowl, mix the apples, oats, maple syrup and walnuts into the yogurt. Sprinkle with wheat germ.

2. Optional-Top with cinnamon and nutmeg Garnish with fresh fruit.

# Raw Granola Breakfast

## INGREDIENTS

- ➢ 6 cups raw oat meal
- ➢ 1 cup sesame seeds
- ➢ 1 cup sunflower seeds
- ➢ 2 tbsp ground flaxseed
- ➢ 1 cup pumpkin seeds
- ➢ 1 cup shredded coconut

- ➢ 1 cup pecans
- ➢ ½ cup wheat germ
- ➢ ⅓ cup maple syrup
- ➢ 1 tbsp flax seed oil
- ➢ 2 tbsp water
- ➢ 1 tsp cinnamon

## DIRECTIONS

1. Whisk together the maple syrup, water, flax seed oil, and cinnamon. Pour over dry ingredients and mix them well with your hands. If you want it sweeter, you can add another tbsp maple syrup, the amount listed is intended only to add gentle sweetness and to bind the granola together.

2. Store in jars. Keep cool. Serve dry (chew thoroughly) or with nut milk. Add a little honey if needed.

# INTERNATIONAL BREAKFAST

# Tea and Fried Egg Sandwich

## INGREDIENTS

- ➤ 4 large eggs
- ➤ 1/4 cup of coconut or olive oil
- ➤ 2 tomatoes nicely chopped
- ➤ Half red onions chopped

- ➤ 1-2 Fresh pepper (spicy pepper)
- ➤ Kosher Salt to taste
- ➤ 1 tsp of grinded crayfish
- ➤ 1 maggi cube (optional)

## DIRECTIONS

1. After heating your frying pan for about a minute, add oil.

2. Add nicely sliced tomato, pepper and onions.

3. Fry for 5-10 minutes and then add a pinch of kosher salt.

4. Finally, add the crayfish.

5. Stir, and then make sure it is spread evenly on the frying pan, add your mixed eggs, do not stir. Leave to cook for a while before you stir.

# Akamu and Akara

**Ingredients you need for Akara**

You need only 5 ingredients to make Akara

## INGREDIENTS

- ➢ 2 cup of Beans
- ➢ 1 habanero peppers (chilli or spicy peppers)

- ➢ half red onion
- ➢ Kosher Salt to taste
- ➢ Canola Oil for frying

## DIRECTIONS

How to make Akamu (know as pap)

1. Place some akamu In a big mixing bowl. Make sure to use a big bowl as the custard grows during preparation.

2. Add a small amount of water to the akamu and stir slowly. Gradually add some water until you have enough mix. Make sure that there are no lumps.

3. Boil some water.

4. When the water is almost boiling, stir the akamu, mix and make sure that nothing has settled at the bottom of the bowl and there is no lump.

5. Slowly and steadily pour the boiled water into the bowl of akamu and stir it simultaneously.

6. Stop stirring only when the akamu starts setting and reduce the amount of water you are pouring until the akamu has completely settled.

7. Stir the custard thoroughly.

8. Add almond milk and honey to taste.

# Yam And Egg Breakfast

## INGREDIENTS

- 10 pieces of Yam (Chopped)
- 2 eggs
- 1 small sized tomato
- 1 scotch Bonnet pepper (ata rodo)
- Handful chopped spring onion
- Handful chopped carrots
- 1 seasoning cube
- 1/4 teaspoon curry
- A Pinch of thyme
- 2 tablespoons of olive or coconut oil
- Salt to taste

## DIRECTIONS

1. In a pot of boiling water, peel and chop your yam and bring to boil. When yam is soft, season with salt and drain the water.

2. In a pan, add all your vegetable and add 2 tablespoon of olive or coconut oil, stir fry all the veggie.

3. In a bowl, whisk your eggs and pour into the frying vegetables. Reduce the heat and allow the eggs cook while stirring it. Increase the heat after a minute and properly stir fry the egg and serve with the yam. For weight watcher, use egg white only

# Chapter 3

# HEALTHY LUNCH

## ENJOY IT

# Eggplant Fufu

**INGREDIENTS FOR EGGPLANT FUFU**

- ➢ 1 medium eggplant
- ➢ 1 teaspoon Psyllium Husk

You can also use Nigerian garden eggs as alternative to eggplants (aubergines). I prefer white garden eggs because they make better looking Garden Egg Fufu than the green ones.

- ➢ 6 garden eggs
- ➢ 1 teaspoon Psyllium Husk

# CAULIFLOWER FUFU

## INGREDIENTS FOR CAULIFLOWER

- ➤ Cauliflower Fufu Combination 1
- ➤ 6 florets cauliflower
- ➤ ½ teaspoon Psyllium Husk

## CAULIFLOWER FUFU COMBINATION 2

- ➤ 6 florets cauliflower
- ➤ ¼ teaspoon Xanthan Gum

# Beef Bulgogi (Korea)

## INGREDIENTS

- 1 pound flank steak, thinly sliced
- 5 tablespoons soy sauce
- 3 tablespoons honey
- ¼ cup chopped green onion
- 2 tablespoons minced garlic
- 2 tablespoons sesame seeds
- 2 tablespoons sesame oil
- ½ teaspoon ground black pepper

## DIRECTIONS

1. Place the beef in a shallow dish. Combine soy sauce, sugar, green onion, garlic, sesame seeds, sesame oil, and ground black pepper in a small bowl. Pour over beef. Cover and refrigerate for at least 1 hour or overnight. 2. Preheat an outdoor grill for high heat, and lightly oil the grate. 3. Quickly grill beef on hot grill until slightly charred and cooked through, 1 to 2 minutes per side.

# CAULIFLOWER PIZZA

## CAULIFLOWER PIZZA

- ➢ 1 medium head cauliflower, cut into florets
- ➢ 1/4 cup grated Parmesan
- ➢ 1 teaspoon Italian seasoning
- ➢ 1/4 teaspoon kosher salt
- ➢ 1 large egg
- ➢ 2 cups freshly grated mozzarella
- ➢ 1/4 cup Spicy Pizza Sauce, recipe follows
- ➢ Fresh basil leaves, for garnish
- ➢ Salad:
- ➢ 4 cups baby greens
- ➢ 2 tablespoons olive oil
- ➢ 1 tablespoon balsamic vinegar
- ➢ Kosher salt and freshly ground black pepper
- ➢ Parmesan shavings, for topping
- ➢ Spicy Pizza Sauce:
- ➢ 1 to 2 tablespoons olive oil
- ➢ 3 cloves garlic, minced
- ➢ 1 medium onion, finely chopped
- ➢ 1/2 cup chicken broth
- ➢ Three 15-ounce cans crushed tomatoes
- ➢ 1 tablespoon brown sugar
- ➢ 1 teaspoon red pepper flakes
- ➢ Kosher salt and freshly ground black pepper

## DIRECTION

Pulse the cauliflower florets in a food processor to a fine snowy powder (you should have about 2 1/2 cups). Transfer the processed cauliflower to a microwave-safe bowl and cover. Microwave until soft, 4 to 6 minutes. Transfer to a clean, dry kitchen towel and allow to cool.

When cool enough to handle, wrap the cauliflower in the towel and wring out as much moisture as possible, transferring to a second towel if necessary. In a large bowl, stir together the cauliflower, Parmesan, Italian seasoning, salt, egg and 1 cup of the mozzarella until well combined. Transfer to the prepared baking sheet and press into a 10-inch round. Bake until golden, 10 to 15 minutes.

Remove the crust from the oven and top with the Spicy Pizza Sauce and remaining 1 cup mozzarella. Bake until the cheese is melted and bubbly, 10 minutes more. Garnish with fresh basil leaves just before serving.

For the salad: Meanwhile, add the greens to a large bowl. Whisk together the olive oil, baslsamic and salt and pepper to taste in a measuring cup. Pour over the greens and toss. Top with Parmesan shavings.

Heat a pan over medium-high heat until hot. Add a tablespoon or so of olive oil, throw in the garlic and chopped onions and give them a stir. Cook until the onions are soft, 4 to 5 minutes. Add the chicken broth, whisking to deglaze the bottom of the pan. Cook until the liquid reduces by half. Add the crushed tomatoes and stir to combine. Add the brown sugar, red pepper flakes and salt and pepper to taste and stir. Bring to a simmer, reduce the heat to low and simmer for 30 minutes. Let cool, then puree the sauce.

# CABBAGE FUFU (SWALLOW)

## INGREDIENTS FOR CAULIFLOWER

You can make Cabbage Fufu with these 2 combinations of ingredients:

### Cabbage Fufu Combination 1

- ➢ 1 small cabbage
- ➢ ½ to 1 teaspoon Psyllium Husk

### CABBAGE FUFU COMBINATION 2

- ➢ 1 small cabbage
- ➢ ¼ teaspoon Xanthan Gum

## RECIPE NOTES

You need to stir thoroughly until the fufu is formed otherwise you might end up with lumps

When the fufu is done, cover it or wrap it in a plastic wrap in order to prevent it from forming a crust. Leave it to cool for few minutes.

# LAYERS SALAD

## INGREDIENT

- ➢ 2 medium bunch lettuce
- ➢ 5 medium carrots
- ➢ 4 small pcs Irish potatoes
- ➢ 2 medium cucumbers

- ➢ 3 medium eggs
- ➢ 1 415g tin Baked Beans in tomato sauce
- ➢ 200g sweet corn
- ➢ 1 red onions

## DIRECTIONS

1. Cut the lettuce into thin shreds.

2. Scrape and shred the carrots using a grater.

3. Peel and cut the boiled potatoes into sizeable cubes.

4. Peel, remove the seeds and cut the cucumber as shown. If you want more green color in your salad, you may peel the cucumber in stripes.

5. Place all the cut vegetables in separate containers.

6. Open the sweet corn and drain the preservation water. Rinse the seeds and set aside. Also open the baked beans tin and set aside. Remove the shells of the hard boiled eggs, slice thinly and set aside.

# Jerk Chicken (Jamaica)

## INGREDIENTS

- 6 green onions, chopped
- 1 onion, chopped
- 1 jalapeno pepper, seeded and minced
- ¾ cup soy sauce
- ½ cup distilled white vinegar
- ¼ cup vegetable oil

- 2 tablespoons organic honey
- 1 tablespoon chopped fresh thyme
- ½ teaspoon ground cloves
- ½ teaspoon ground nutmeg
- ½ teaspoon ground allspice
- 1 ½ pounds skinless, boneless chicken breast halves

## DIRECTIONS

1. In a food processor or blender, combine the green onions, onion, jalapeno pepper, soy sauce, vinegar, olive oil, brown sugar, thyme, cloves, nutmeg and allspice. Mix for about 15 seconds.

2. Place the chicken in a medium bowl, and coat with the marinade. Refrigerate for 4 to 6 hours, or overnight.

3. Preheat grill for high heat.

4. Lightly oil grill grate. Cook chicken on the prepared grill 6 to 8 minutes, until juices run clear. 4 serving

# FRIED RICE

## INGREDIENTS

- 3 cups of regular long grain rice
- ½-1 cup of raw green beans(chopped)
- ¼ cup of whole kernel corn
- ¼ cup fresh sweet peas(optional)
- ½ cup of carrots (chopped or sliced)
- 1 cup of cabbage (thinly sliced)
- ½ cup of minced or sliced onion
- 1stalk of green onion(sliced)
- 3 small minced garlic cloves(optional)
- one slab of beef liver
- ½-1lb of raw or cooked shrimp.

- 1small chicken breast (optional in notesil)
- ½ tbsp. of thyme
- 1 bay leaf
- 3tsps. green curry powder
- ¼tsp black pepper
- ⅛tsp nut meg
- 1½-2 cups of chicken stock
- 4½ tbsps. of peanut or ground nut oil
- 1 knob of butter
- salt to taste
- bouillon

## INSTRUCTIONS

### PREP

1. Wash liver and boil with salt and onion until tender; then drain and chop into small bite sizes and set aside.

2. Wash rice under running Luke warm water until clear; then drain.

3. Pour 2 tbsps. of oil into a cooking pot, add a bay leaf into the oil, add the rice then stir fry for about 3 minutes or until the rice begins to pop. Meanwhile, add 2tsps. of the curry powder and combine for about another minute. Pour the meat stock just to the top of the

rice, you do not have to use up the meat stock if it is too much) (season if using water) Cook the rice until aldonate (not too hard and not too soft). Once the rice is done, fluff with a fork and refrigerate for an hour or more (This helps to remove the moisture and helps with easy handling without causing it to be mushy) If you cannot refrigerate the rice, just pour it onto a flat tray and air it out

## METHOD

1. In a wok and on high heat, heat up 1tbsp of the peanut oil. Pour in the chopped liver and sauté until golden brown. Drain the cooked liver unto a paper towel and set aside. (Wipe the wok)

2. Pour in the remaining oil into the wok and let it get hot; then pour in the onion and garlic. Sauté until the onion is translucent and the garlic is fragrant. Add the thyme and remaining curry along with a bouillon if using. (Be ready to go through frying the vegetables and the rice quickly)

3. Throw in your green beans along with the other vegetables except the green onion... stir fry quickly for about 2 minutes (You want the vegetables to retain it's crunch). Mix in the shrimp and liver. Season with a little salt and black pepper. Pour in the rice in little increments and keep stirring really fast. Once the rice is mixed in, stir in the nutmeg and the green onion and check for seasonings; making sure to adjust the seasonings where necessary. Stir in the butter. Remove rice from the heat and serve

# Chilean-Style Sopaipillas (Chile)

## INGREDIENTS

- 9 ounces zapallo squash
- 4 ¼ cups all-purpose flour
- 1 teaspoon baking soda

- 1 teaspoon salt butter, melted
- 2 cups olive or coconut oil for pan-frying
- 10 tablespoons

## DIRECTIONS

1. Peel, seed, and cut the zapallo into chunks. Place in a saucepan, cover with water, and bring to a boil over medium-high heat. Cook until zapallo is soft and easily pierced with a fork, 15 to 20 minutes. Drain and allow to cool slightly.

2. Mix the flour, baking soda, and salt together in a mixing bowl, and set aside. Stir together the squash and melted butter. Stir the flour mixture into the butter mixture until blended. Turn the dough out onto a lightly floured surface and knead until soft and satiny, adding a little more flour if necessary. Cover dough with a towel and allow to rest 15 minutes.

3. Roll out the dough to 1/8 inch thick, and cut into 3 inch diameter circles. Poke each circle a few times with a fork to make holes and prevent rising. 4. Pour vegetable oil into a large, deep skillet and heat over medium-high heat until hot, 385 degrees F (195 degrees C). Place several of the dough circles into hot oil; cook until lightly browned, 3 to 4 minutes. Drain on paper towels.

4. 9 Servings

# Vegetarian Tortilla Stew (Mexico)

## INGREDIENTS

- 1 (19 ounce) can green enchilada sauce
- 1 ½ cups water
- 11. 1 cube vegetable bouillon (optional, use blended crayfish)
- ½ teaspoon garlic powder
- ¼ teaspoon chili powder
- 1 ¼ teaspoon ground cumin

- ½ (16 ounce) can diced tomatoes
- 1 cup frozen corn
- ½ cup vegetarian chicken substitute, diced (optional)
- (6 inch) corn tortillas, torn into strips
- 1 tablespoon chopped fresh cilantro
- Salt and pepper to taste

## DIRECTIONS

1. In a pot, mix the enchilada sauce and water. Dissolve the bouillon cube or grinded crayfish in the liquid, and season with garlic powder, chile powder, and cumin. Bring to a boil, and reduce heat to low. Mix in the beans, tomatoes, and corn. Simmer until heated through. Mix in vegetarian chicken and tortillas, and cook until heated through. Stir in cilantro, and season with salt and pepper to serve. 4 Servings

# Spinach with Garbanzo Beans Recipe (Spain)

## INGREDIENTS

- 1 tablespoon extra-virgin olive oil
- 4 cloves garlic, minced 1/2 onion, diced
- 1 (10 ounce) box frozen chopped spinach, thawed and drained well
- 1 (12 ounce) can garbanzo beans, drained
- ½ teaspoon cumin
- ½ teaspoon salt

## DIRECTIONS

1. Rub coconut oil in a skillet over medium-low heat. Cook the garlic and onion in the oil until translucent, about 5 minutes. Stir in the spinach, garbanzo beans, cumin, and salt. Use your stirring spoon to lightly mash the beans as the mixture cooks. Allow to cook until thoroughly heated. 4 Servings

# Asparagus Cashew Rice Pilaf (Armenia)

## INGREDIENTS

- ¼ cup butter
- 2 ounces uncooked spaghetti, broken
- ¼ cup minced onion
- ½ teaspoon minced garlic
- 1 ¼ cups uncooked jasmine rice
- 2 ¼ cups vegetable broth
- salt and pepper to taste
- ½ pound fresh asparagus, trimmed and cut into 2 inch pieces
- ½ cup cashew halves

## DIRECTIONS

1. Melt butter in a medium saucepan over medium-low heat. Increase heat to medium, and stir in spaghetti, cooking until coated with the melted butter and lightly browned.

2. Stir onion and garlic into the saucepan, and cook about 2 minutes, until tender. Stir in jasmine rice, and cook about 5 minutes. Pour in vegetable broth. Season mixture with salt and pepper. Bring the mixture to a boil, cover, and cook 20 minutes, until rice is tender and liquid has been absorbed.

3. Place asparagus in a separate medium saucepan with enough water to cover. Bring to a boil, and cook until tender but firm.

4. Mix asparagus and cashew halves into the rice mixture, and serve warm. 8 Servings

# Steamed Mussels with Fennel, Tomatoes, Ouzo, and Cream (Greece)

## INGREDIENTS

- 1 tablespoon olive oil
- 2 shallots, finely chopped
- 4 cloves garlic, finely chopped
- 1 bulb fennel - trimmed, cored and thinly sliced
- 1 large tomato, cubed
- ½ cup white wine

- ¼ cup ouzo
- ½ cup heavy cream
- 4 pounds mussels, cleaned and debearded
- ⅓ cup fresh basil leaves, torn
- salt to taste

## DIRECTIONS

1. Rub your coconut oil in a medium saucepan over medium heat. Stir in shallots and garlic, and cook until tender. Stir in fennel and tomato, and continue cooking about 5 minutes.

2. Mix white wine, ouzo, and heavy cream into the saucepan, and bring to a boil. Gradually stir in mussels, 1/2 the basil, and salt.

3. Cover saucepan, and continue cooking about 5 minutes, until the mussels have opened. Garnish with remaining basil to serve. 4 Servings

# JOLLOF RICE

## INGREDIENTS

Makes: a family-sized pot  Prep time: 30 min  Cook time: 1 hrs 30 min

- 4 cups uncooked long-grain rice (not basmati)
- 6 cups stock (vegetable, chicken, or beef) or water, divided
- 6 medium-sized fresh plum/Roma tomatoes, chopped, OR a 400-gram tin of tomatoes
- 6 fresh, red poblano peppers (or 4 large red bell peppers), seeds discarded
- 3 medium-sized red onions (1 sliced thinly, 2 roughly chopped), divided
- 1 Scotch bonnet peppers (yellow is my favorite!), to taste
- 1/3 cup oil (vegetable/ canola/coconut, not olive oil)
- 3 tablespoons tomato paste
- 2 teaspoons curry powder
- 1 teaspoon (heaping) dried thyme
- 2 dried bay leaves
- 2 teaspoons unsalted butter (optional), divided
- 1 dash Salt, to taste

Rinse the rice to get rid of some starch then parboil: Bring the rice to a boil with 2 cups of the stock (or water) then cook on medium heat, covered, about 12 to 15 minutes. Rice will still be hard, a bit "white" (not translucent) and only partly cooked. Remove from the heat and set aside.

In a blender, combine tomatoes, red poblano (or bell) peppers, chopped onions, and chile pepper; blend till smooth, about a minute or two. You should have roughly 4 cups of blended mix.

In a large pan, heat oil and add sliced onion. Season with a pinch of salt, stir-fry for a minute or two, then add the tomato paste, curry powder, dried thyme and bay leaves. Stir for another 2 minutes. Add the blended tomato-pepper-chile mixture, stir, and set on medium heat for 10 to 12 minutes so the mix cooks and the raw taste of the tomatoes is gone. You might feel your eyes sting with onions.

Add 2 cups of the stock to the cooked tomato sauce, 1 teaspoon of butter, and then add the parboiled rice. Stir, cover with a double piece of foil/ baking or parchment paper and put a lid on the pan. This will seal in the steam and lock in the flavour. Cook on low heat for 15 minutes. Stir again, adjust seasoning to taste, then add the remaining 1 cup of stock. Stir, cover with foil/ baking or parchment paper and let cook for another 15 to 20 minutes, stirring every 10 minutes or so to prevent burning and till the rice is cooked and the grains are separate.

Don't be afraid to add some more stock or water—by the half-cup, stirring gently—if you find it a bit hard. When it's cooked, take off heat and remove the cover of the pot. Put a tea cloth over the top and leave for half an hour or more, till ready to serve.

To make Party Rice, you'll need one more step. Now Party Rice is essentially Smoky Jollof Rice, traditionally cooked over an open fire. However, you can achieve the same results on the stove top. Here's how: Once the rice is cooked, turn up the heat with the lid on and leave to "burn" for 3 to 5 minutes. You'll hear the rice crackled and snap and it will smell toasted. Turn off the heat and leave with the lid on to "rest" till ready to serve. The longer the lid stays on, the smokier. Let the party begin!

**PARTY JOILOF RICE**

**INGREDIENTS:**

- ➤ 4 Cups Easy Cook Rice
- ➤ 3 Large/ 4 Medium Red Bell Peppers (Tatashe)
- ➤ 1/2 Can of Plum Tomatoes/ 2 Medium Size Tomatoes
- ➤ 11/2 Scotch Bonnet (Ata Rodo)
- ➤ 2 cups Beef or Chicken Stock
- ➤ 120g Tomato Paste
- ➤ 2 Onions
- ➤ 100ml /6 Tablespoons Cooking oil
- ➤ 2 Tablespoons Butter
- ➤ 1 Tablespoon Minced Ginger
- ➤ 1/2 Teaspoon Curry powder and Thyme
- ➤ 1/2 Teaspoon any seasoning of your choosing
- ➤ 3 Knorr Chicken cubes
- ➤ 2 Teaspoons White pepper
- ➤ 3 Bay Leaves

# Mansaka (Traditional Casserole from Denmark)

## INGREDIENTS

- 1 tablespoon shortening
- 1 ½ pounds ground beef
- 2 cups sliced onion
- 1 clove garlic, minced
- 1 tablespoon all-purpose flour
- 1 ½ teaspoons salt
- ¼ teaspoon ground black pepper
- 1 teaspoon sugar

- 1 teaspoon dried basil
- ½ teaspoon ground cinnamon
- ½ teaspoon dried oregano
- 1 (4 ounce) can mushrooms, drained
- 1 (15 ounce) can tomato sauce
- 4 potatoes, thinly sliced
- 1 cup shredded Swiss cheese

## DIRECTIONS

1. Melt the shortening in a large skillet over medium-high heat. Add the ground beef, and cook, stirring to crumble, until evenly browned. Mix in the onion and garlic; cook until tender. Drain excess grease, and sprinkle in the flour, salt, pepper, sugar, basil, cinnamon and oregano. Stir in the mushrooms and tomato sauce, and simmer for 15 minutes over low heat.Meanwhile, place the potatoes in a microwave-safe bowl or dish, and cook for 5 to 6 minutes, stirring occasionally, or until about halfway done.

2. Preheat the oven to 350 degrees F (175 degrees C). In the bottom of a 9x13 inch baking dish, or shallow casserole dish of similar size, layer half of the potatoes. Spread half of the meat sauce over them, then sprinkle with half of the cheese. Repeat the layers ending with cheese on top.

3. Bake for 35 minutes in the preheated oven, until potatoes are tender and cheese is browned.

**DO NOT FORGET TO ADD GINGER AND GARLIC TO YOUR FOOD**

# Green Veggie Energy Drink

## INGREDIENTS

- ➢ 4 Leaves Romaine lettuce
- ➢ 1 small bunch of spinach
- ➢ 1 small bunch of parsley
- ➢ Dandelion greens to taste

- ➢ 3 stalks of celery
- ➢ 2 large apples, cored
- ➢ Fresh mint leaf to taste

## DIRECTIONS

1. One at a time, roll the romaine lettuce, spinach, parsley and dandelion greens into a tight ball and push them through the juicer

2. Push the celery and apple through juicer: you can then garnish your energy booster with mint

# African Peanut Soup Recipe

## INGREDIENTS

- 2 tablespoons olive oil
- 2 medium onions, chopped
- 2 large red bell peppers, chopped
- 4 cloves garlic, minced
- 1 (28 ounce) can crushed tomatoes, with liquid

- 8 cups vegetable broth or stock
- ¼ teaspoon pepper
- ¼ teaspoon chili powder (optional)
- ⅔ cup extra crunchy peanut butter
- ½ cup uncooked brown rice

## DIRECTIONS

1. Cook onions and bell peppers until lightly browned and tender, stirring in garlic when almost done to prevent burning. Stir in tomatoes, vegetable stock, pepper, and chili powder. Reduce heat to low and simmer, uncovered, for 30 minutes. Stir in rice, cover, and simmer another fifteen minutes or until rice is tender. Stir in peanut butter until well blended, and serve. 10 servings

# Chicken Cordon Bleu Recipe

## INGREDIENTS

- 6 skinless, boneless chicken breast halves
- 6 slices Swiss cheese
- 6 slices ham
- 3 tablespoons all-purpose flour
- 1 teaspoon paprika
- 6 tablespoons butter
- ½ cup dry white wine
- 1 teaspoon chicken bouillon granules
- 1 tablespoon cornstarch
- 1 cup heavy whipping cream

## DIRECTIONS

1. Pound chicken breasts if they are too thick. Place a cheese and ham slice on each breast within 1/2 inch of the edges. Fold the edges of the chicken over the filling, and secure with toothpicks. Mix the flour and paprika in a small bowl, and coat the chicken pieces Heat the butter in a large skillet over medium-high heat, and cook the chicken until browned on all sides. Add the wine and bouillon. Reduce heat to low, cover, and simmer for 30 minutes, until chicken is no longer pink and juices run clear. Remove the toothpicks, and transfer the breasts to a warm platter. Blend the cornstarch with the cream in a small bowl, and whisk slowly into the skillet. Cook, stirring until thickened, and pour over the chicken. Serve warm.

# Milk Tart (South Africa)

## INGREDIENTS

- ½ cup butter, softened
- 1 cup white sugar
- 1 egg
- 2 cups all-purpose flour
- 2 teaspoons baking powder
- 1 pinch salt
- 4 cups milk

- 1 teaspoon vanilla extract
- 1 tablespoon butter
- 2 ½ tablespoons all-purpose flour
- 2 ½ tablespoons cornstarch
- ½ cup white sugar
- 2 eggs, beaten
- ½ teaspoon ground cinnamon

## DIRECTIONS

1. Preheat oven to 350 degrees F (175 degrees C). In a medium mixing bowl, cream together 1/2 cup butter or margarine and 1 cup sugar. Add 1 egg and beat until mixture is smooth. In a separate bowl, mix together 2 cups flour, baking powder, and salt. Stir flour mixture into sugar mixture just until ingredients are thoroughly combined. Press mixture into bottom and sides of two 9-inch pie pans. 3. Bake in preheated oven for 10 to 15 minutes, until golden brown. 4. In a large saucepan, combine milk, vanilla extract, and 1 tablespoon butter or margarine. Bring to a boil over medium heat, then remove from burner. 5. In a separate bowl, mix together 2 1/2 tablespoons flour, cornstarch, and 1/2 cup sugar. Add beaten eggs to sugar mixture and whisk until smooth. Slowly whisk mixture into milk. Return pan to heat and bring to a boil, stirring constantly. Boil and stir 5 minutes. Pour half of mixture into each pastry shell. Sprinkle with cinnamon. Chill before serving. 16 servings.

# Cabbage Dish (From Ethiopian)

## INGREDIENTS

- ½ cup olive oil
- 4 carrots, thinly sliced
- 1 onion, thinly sliced
- 1 teaspoon sea salt
- ½ teaspoon ground black pepper
- ½ teaspoon ground cumin
- ¼ teaspoon ground turmeric
- 1/2 head cabbage, shredded
- 5 potatoes, peeled and cut into 1-inch cubes

## DIRECTIONS

1. Heat the olive oil in a skillet over medium heat. Cook the carrots and onion in the hot oil about 5 minutes. Stir in the salt, pepper, cumin, turmeric, and cabbage and cook another 15 to 20 minutes. Add the potatoes; cover. Reduce heat to medium-low and cook until potatoes are soft, 20 to 30 minutes. 5 servings

# Pancit Canton (Philippine Breakfast)

## INGREDIENTS

- 1 pack 250 grams pancit canton (flour noodles)
- 4 ounces pork thinly sliced
- 1 piece Chinese style sausage sliced
- 1 small onion sliced
- 1 teaspoon minced garlic
- 8 to 10 pieces medium shrimp
- 10 to 12 pieces snap peas or snow peas
- ¾ cup carrot julienne
- 1 head small cabbage chopped
- 1 ½ cups chicken broth
- 1 tablespoon oyster sauce optional
- 3 tablespoons soy sauce
- ¾ cup water
- ½ cup chopped flat leaf parsley
- 3 tablespoons cooking oil
- Salt and pepper to taste

## DIRECTIONS

1. Place 2 cups of ice and 3 cups water in a large bowl. Set aside.Boil 6 cups of water in a cooking pot. Once the water starts to boil, blanch the snap peas, carrots, and cabbage for 35 to 50 seconds. Quickly remove the vegetables and immerse in bowl with ice cold water. Drain the water after 2 minutes and set aside.

2. Heat a large wok or cooking pot and pour-in the cooking oil. Saute the onion and garlic. Add the pork and sausage slices and continue to cook for 2 minutes. Add-in soy sauce and oyster sauce. Stir.Pour-in chicken broth and water. Add salt and pepper. Let boil. continue to cook for 5 to 10 minutes.

3. Put-in the shrimp and parsley. Cook for 3 minutes. Add more water if needed.

4. Put-in the flour noodles. Gently toss until the noodles absorb the liquid.Add-in the blanched vegetables. Toss and cook for 1 to 2 minutes.Transfer to a serving plate. Serve. Share and enjoy!

# Infection Fighting Lemon Garlic Drink

## INGREDIENTS

- 1 lemon
- 1-2 garlic buds
- 2cups of water
- 1 tbsp sweetener

## DIRECTIONS

Using a peeler take off only the yellow part of the rind of the lemon, leaving the white part with it's Vitamin C complex. Cut lemon in half with the seeds and throw in the blender. Put yellow lemon peelings in a ziploc bag in the freezer (use one inch when you make a fruit smoothie for a nice lemon taste). Throw in garlic and water and blend well. The strong lemon and garlic flavors mellow each other out for an easily drinkable therapeutic treat.

This is a powerful healing drink, take 1/2 tsp of cayenne and 1/3 cup water, mix and drink quickly before the lemon

# Healthy EFORIRO (Yoruba Nigeria)

One of the most favorite Filipino breakfast is Bangusilo which is a combination of fried breaded bangus, Sinangag rice, and a sunny side up egg

## INGREDIENTS FOR EFO RIRO

- ➢ 400g or two bunches of Spinach Vegetable / Efo tete.
- ➢ Blended pepper with onions.
- ➢ 5 or more Fresh Tomatoes
- ➢ 8 or more some Red Chilli Peppers
- ➢ Boiled Seasoned Crab / Snails / Shrimps-

- ➢ Boiled and seasoned assorted Meat (Beef parts)
- ➢ Smoked Stock Fish
- ➢ Dry Stock Fish
- ➢ Periwinkle
- ➢ 300 ml Palm oil
- ➢ Maggi/Salt or other seasoning

## DIRECTIONS

STEP 1 Fry four cooking spoons of palm oil in a deep cooking pan, slice onions and add salt, then leave for 2mins.

STEP 2 Add the blended pepper, small red chilli pepper, ½ a clove of chopped garlic and ginger and cook for 10 minutes.

STEP 3 Add all the ingredients, sliced tomatoes , boiled beef, Cray fish, stock dry fish, assorted meat, shrimps, crab, snail and seasoned, add periwinkle.

STEP 4 Add the Spinach vegetable and cook for a further 2-3mins stir together. Serve Efo Riro vegetable soup with Eba, Fufu, Amala or Pounded yam.

## INGREDIENTS FOR EFO RIRO WITHOUT PERIWINKLES AND SNAIL

- 2kg Shoko/ Spinach leaves(about 8 wraps if you buy in Nigerian market)
- 250 gr Assorted Meat (tripe,cow skin(ponmo), beef)
- 250 gr Assorted Fish (stock fish, smoked fish)
- 3 Fresh Tomatoes or 2 Bell peppers(tatashe)
- 2 Scotch Bonnets Peppers (atarodo)
- 1 teaspoon Iru /dawadawa/ogiri (fermented locust beans ) (optional)
- 1- 2 Cooking-spoonful Palm oil
- 1 medium sized onions
- 1 tablespoonful Ground crayfish
- 2 stock cubes
- Salt to tasteCooking Method

Before cooking Efo Riro Soup, pick and wash the vegetables;shred/cut into tiny bits. To get less liquid in the soup,you can blanch the vegetables and set side.

Wash the assorted meat and fish. De-bone the smoked fish, and set all aside.** Blend the peppers and tomatoes, and set aside,Now to cook the soup...

1. Season and cook the assorted meat and fish with onions, one stock cube, a little salt and other seasoning of choice. Remember to cook the tougher meat first(in my case;tripe(shaki) Cook until the liquid in the pot is well absorbed(dried up) and the meat and stock fish are tender .

2. In another dry pot, heat up the palm oil, until it begins to smoke a little. Add the ground tomatoes & peppers and fry until the mixture loses its sour taste; this takes about 15-20minutes.3. Now add the cooked meat & fish. Add ground iru, ground crayfish and stock cube. Mix thoroughly, cover and leave to boil for 10 minutes.4. After 10 minutes, add the vegetables and salt to taste. Mix well and leave to simmer for 5 minutes and your delicious Efo Riro soup is ready.

# Moi Moi (Baked Bean)

## INGREDIENTS

Moimoi (beans cake)

Moi Moi, so tasty they named it twice. Okay that was a bit corny but I love this dish made from beans/black eyed peas. I think it makes an excellent Saturday morning breakfast because it is highly nutritious whilst filling. Serve with custard or if throwing a party alongside Jollof rice.

## INGREDIENTS

Serves 4

- ➢ 500g Beans/Black Eyed Peas.
- ➢ 4 Boiled Eggs (optional)
- ➢ 2 ½ cooking spoons of Palm oil/ Vegetable oil
- ➢ Cooked Fish/Sardines
- ➢ ½ Clove Garlic/Ginger

- ➢ 60g Shrimps (optional)
- ➢ Leaves/Sandwich bags/Aluminium cups.
- ➢ 4 Fresh Tomatoes
- ➢ 7 Small Chilli Pepper
- ➢ Maggi/Salt

## DIRECTIONS

STEP 1 Soak the Beans/Black eyed peas for not longer than 30 – 45 minutes, wash and peel off the brown back of the beans by rubbing the beans with your palms until it becomes white then wash thoroughly. Be sure to remove all the brown peels.

STEP 2 Wash the beans till all is clean white, add onions, red chilli pepper, tomatoes, chopped small garlic and a bit of ginger (very little), blend all together.

STEP 3 Boil the eggs, shrimps and fish

STEP 4 Add 2 ½ tablespoon of palm oil or vegetable oil and seasoning like Maggi/salt then stir, taste if seasoning is okay.

STEP 5 Slice the egg and shred the fish make sure to remove the bones.

STEP 6 Rinse the leave/sandwich bag/aluminium cups, fold into a cone brake the bottom backward to avoid leakage, pour the grounded beans, add few shrimps, fresh sliced eggs and wrap the leave.

STEP 7 Put water in a cooking pan and add all the wraps inside cover to cook for 30mins.

STEP 8 Open one wrap to see if cooked and solid.

Note: Instead of leaves use sandwich bags or aluminium cups.

Tip: Make aluminium cups by cutting open cans of condensed or evaporated milk.

Use palm oil instead of Vegetable oil with enough large red peppers to improve the richness and reddishness of Moi Moi, which makes it more appetising.

# CONCLUSION

We hope you enjoyed the healthy food recipes in this publication. Eating a high-fiber and low carb diet can help you lose weight and lower cholesterol levels and prevent constipation. For more information and to subscribe to our Healthy Menu, visit our website www.ultragc.com for easily plan healthy breakfasts, lunches, dinners and snacks with help from ULTRA HEALTHY LIVING

ENJOY! ENJOY!ENJOY IT

Printed in the United States
By Bookmasters